Telephones

Written by
Jill Atkins

Did you know that a hundred and fifty years ago, nobody had a telephone?

Why not?

Because telephones hadn't been invented yet!

Then some extremely clever people raced to be the first to invent equipment that could send sounds along a wire.

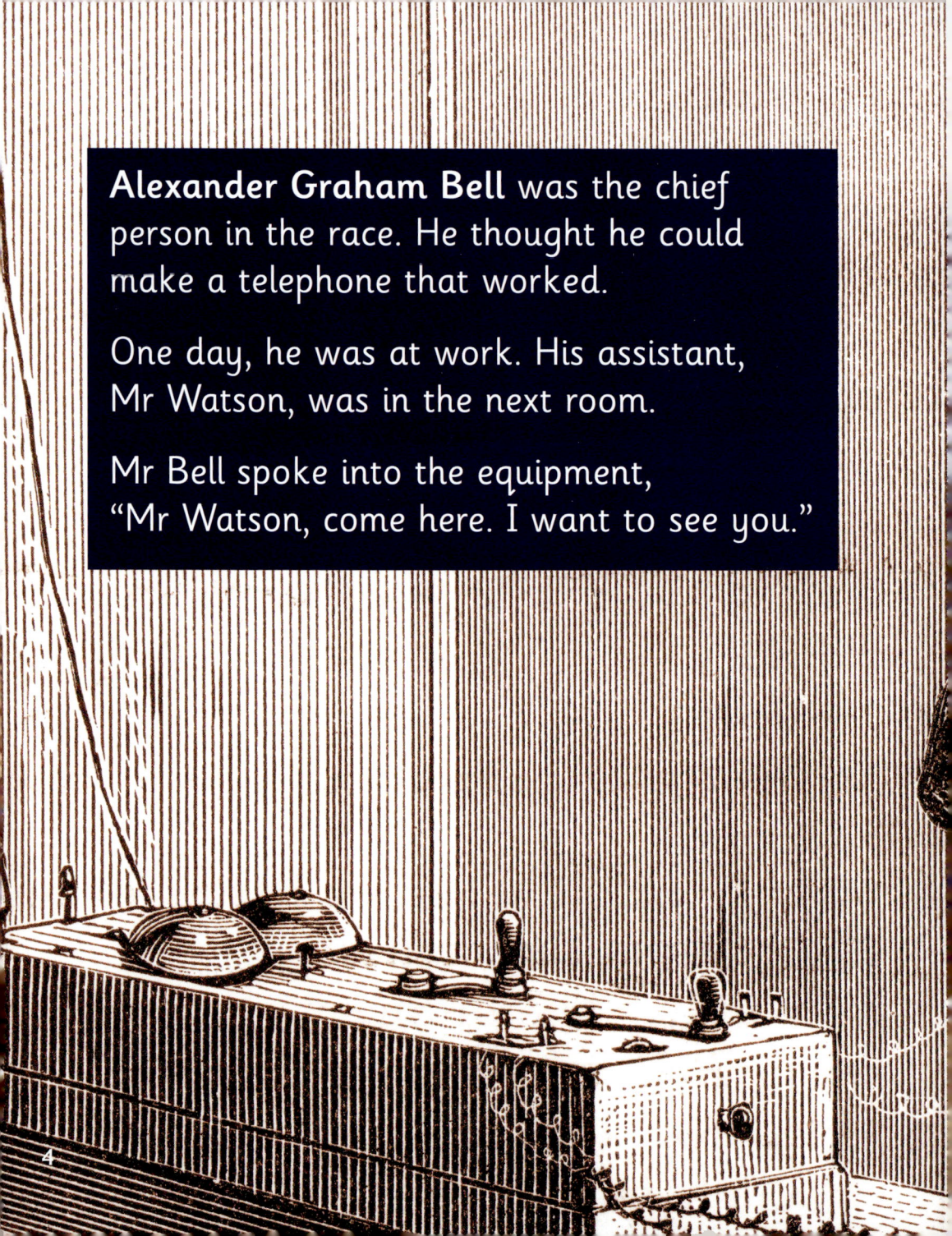

Alexander Graham Bell was the chief person in the race. He thought he could make a telephone that worked.

One day, he was at work. His assistant, Mr Watson, was in the next room.

Mr Bell spoke into the equipment, "Mr Watson, come here. I want to see you."

With his equipment in the next room, Mr Watson heard Mr Bell talking in his ear – and went to see him.

That was a big relief for Mr Bell and it made him very happy. He had found the key to the problem!

Very soon, people heard about this fantastic equipment, but it took many years to develop a telephone that could be used by everyone.

Many people wanted a telephone, but they cost a lot of money, so only rich people could afford one.

These are some early telephones.

You had to put your finger in the hole for each number you needed, like this. It took a long time to make a call. You had to know the telephone number of the person you were calling, as well!

These phones were next!

Not many people had a phone, so you might have to use a phone in a public phone box. You had to put money in a slot to make the phone work.

You had to pay extra money if you talked for too long!

Then these phones were invented. Now you just had to press the numbers to make a call.

But you still had to know the telephone number of the person you wanted to speak to!

The first mobile phones came with a heavy box.

They were useful, but it was hard work to carry them around with you.

Soon, mobile phones like these were made. They were still very big, but not as heavy as the older ones.

These mobile phones could remember the numbers of people you called.

Slowly, the people that made phones began to make them smaller.

See how different they began to look.

Now mobile phones are flat and slim. They are not so heavy.

People can text or take photos or speak to their friends.

Do you think phones have changed a lot since they were invented, nearly a hundred and fifty years ago?

Did you know you can make your own kind of phone? You just use a pair of tins and a length of string.

You can talk to each other along the string! Why don't you try it?